16.99

Let's Take Care of Our New Fish

Alejandro Algarra / Rosa M. Curto

BARRON'S

A visit to the aquarium

Last Saturday, Maria and her brother Paul went to the aquarium. What pretty fish they saw there, of all different shapes and colors! Some were large and swam quickly between the rocks. Others, like the sea horse, were more slender and moved more slowly. The children enjoyed the visit very much, and they have been thinking about something for the last few days.

A pretty colored fish

"Mom! Maria and I have had an idea. Let's see what you think", said Paul. "What is your idea?" asked mom. "We liked the visit to the aquarium very much, and we thought that we'd also like to have a fish here at home." Mom agreed, and Paul and Maria jumped for joy. Then they had to decide what kind of fish they wanted. After talking to a friend, they decided to get a goldfish. It's a freshwater fish with very pretty colors, and it's easy to look after if you follow some simple rules.

About the aquarium

You must follow several guidelines regarding the aquarium for the goldfish to feel comfortable. Before the children choose which one they want, they have to prepare the aquarium and its accessories:

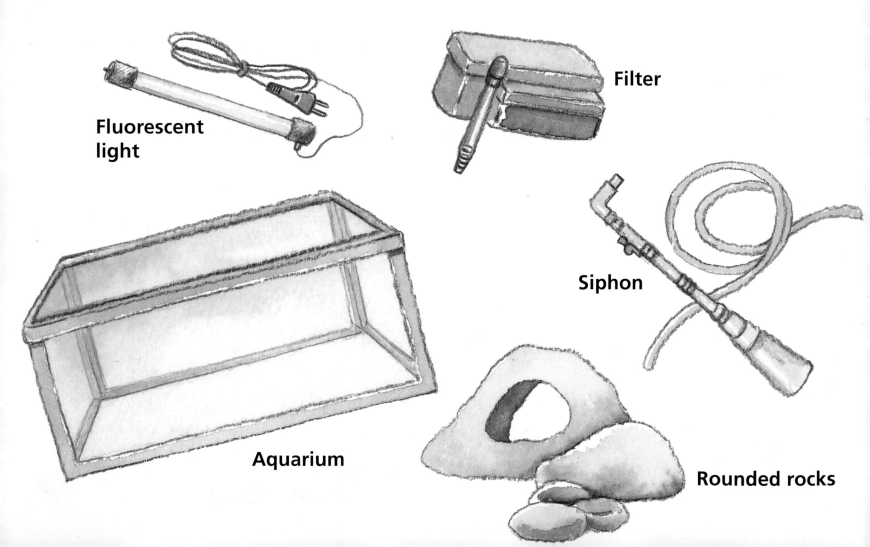

Fluorescent light

Filter

Siphon

Aquarium

Rounded rocks

- Aquarium: It should always be rectangular; never use a goldfish bowl. For goldfish, the minimum size is 10 gallons (30 L), but a 20-gallon (76 L) aquarium would be better.
- Filtration and aeration system: The filter should be powerful enough to clean the aquarium. The aeration system produces a stream of bubbles that oxygenates the water.
- Gravel: Place about 2 inches (5 cm) of dark, not very thick gravel in the aquarium.
- Plants: They should be abundant and hardy, as the goldfish loves to eat greens. They should be planted in the gravel.
- Decoration: Some rounded stones and a branch or decoration where it can take shelter. Such items should always be purchased from an aquarium or pet store.
- A cover for the aquarium and a light: You can use fluorescent bulbs.

Trunk

Gravel

Plants, algae

Choosing our goldfish

Paul and Maria went to the pet store with Dad. They had to choose a goldfish to take home. They saw a little one they liked and asked Dad if he thought it was all right. "It's very pretty!" said Dad. The children loved its colors: It was white with orange patches on its head and body. The storekeeper told them it was a "comet" goldfish and that it was a very good choice.

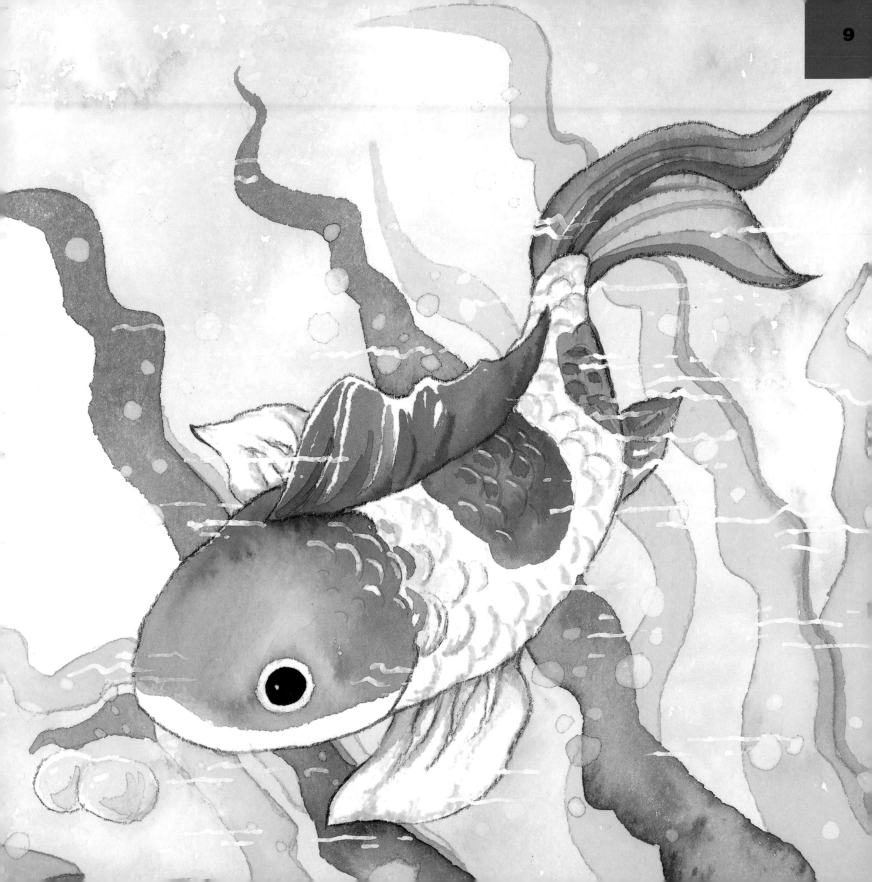

Welcome!

On the way home, Maria was thinking of a good name for their new pet. She wanted to call it "Goldie" and Paul agreed. When they arrived home, the children took the bag with the fish and placed it inside the aquarium, so that Goldie

could get used to his new home. After half an hour, Mom used a small net to take the fish out of the bag, to avoid mixing the water from the store with that of the aquarium. Everything had been ready for several days: the water, gravel, plants, and decoration. Now the fish could swim in its new world.

A very curious fish

Goldie appears to love the aquarium. He swims quickly between the plants and hides behind the branch, and then he swims up to the stream of bubbles coming out of the filter. During the first few days, he got scared when he approached the glass or when they took the cover off to feed him. He hid behind a branch and waited for a while until he felt safer. "Why does he hide?" asked Maria. "Because he doesn't know us yet!" Paul told her. "You'll see how quickly he gets used to you."

It's lunchtime!

Goldie should be fed twice a day, and he likes to eat once in the morning. When the children come home from school, the aquarium light is already turned on. It's a good time to feed their fish. Maria takes a pinch of flakes and sprinkles them in the aquarium while Paul holds the cover. Fish love to eat. They would eat all day if they could. Goldie devoured the flakes in a couple of minutes. But the children should not be deceived: It's enough food for this meal. If they gave Goldie more, he would get sick from indigestion. Anyway, he has some plants to feed on in the aquarium, and they sometimes give him some boiled spinach.

Fresh lettuce

Boiled spinach

Snowflakes

Pellets with nutrients

He's not scared any more!

Goldie is gradually getting used to the presence of the children.
He doesn't hide anymore when they go near the aquarium.
One day, Maria gave him a great surprise. She offered him a
piece of boiled spinach, and Goldie came up to the surface and
nibbled the greens without fear. "Look, Dad! The little fish isn't
scared of us any more!" shouted Maria happily.

A very clever fish

Paul had always been told that fish were not very smart and that they have no memory. He knows that this isn't true, at least not for Goldie. Paul has noticed that the fish recognizes him and Maria perfectly. When one of them goes up to the aquarium, Goldie starts swimming quickly round the tank and goes up to the glass, asking for food. He even goes to the surface and opens his mouth to see whether the children are going to give him some food. It appears that he can even distinguish their voices! On the other hand, when some friends come around, the fish stays among the plants without paying attention.

Cleaning tasks

It's important to keep the aquarium clean and change some of the water. If we didn't do so, our little fish's poops would accumulate and not even the filter would be able to clean the water well. Every week, with the help of Mom and Dad, Paul removes 20 percent of the water with a special siphon. The bucket he uses is only used for adding the water to Goldie's tank. The siphon is also used for removing some of the remains that dirty the gravel. Meanwhile, Maria passes a magnet over the glass to clean off the excess algae. Then they add tap water at the same temperature, plus a few drops of conditioner, refilling it to the same level as before.

A new friend

Paul and Maria are very happy with their goldfish, which is why they asked for a companion for Goldie shortly afterwards. "Don't you think he feels very lonely?" asked Maria. "Well, what do you think we should do?" replied Dad, smiling. "…Mmm, I think we should bring him a new little fish to play with and share this large aquarium," she said. The following afternoon, Dad arrived home with a bag of water with a goldfish inside it. "Great!" shouted Maria and Paul excitedly.

Little friends

The new fish is about the same size as Goldie. It is white and its shiny scales can be seen very clearly. For the first few days, Goldie chased it and seemed to bite its fins, but then he got used to it, and now they swim everywhere together. Maria gave the new fish a name: It's called "Whitey." How pretty their long tails are when they're together in the middle of the aquarium!

A happy surprise

Some time has gone by and the two fish are very happy in their aquarium. A few days ago, they took the whole family by surprise: Goldie is a female and Whitey is a male. The children realized this after he had been chasing her for a few days and Goldie scattered some eggs around the aquarium and these stuck to the plants. Afterward, Whitey fertilized them and two or three days later, some tiny fish appeared. Many of them were eaten by their parents, but some survived. Paul collected them very carefully and placed them in a special tank for raising "baby" fish. This is a large family!

Don't do that!

A few days ago, Paul found out that a friend of his had let go some fish that he had in his house. He had put them in a pond near the school. "You should never do that. Even if you get fed up with your fish, the last things you should do is to let them go or destroy them," Paul told him when he found out. "So what should I do if I don't want them any more?" asked his friend. "It's easy: You can take them to a store so they can find a new owner to take care of them. Some fish, like the goldfish, can live for many years!"

The joy of the house

Since they arrived at the house, Goldie and Whitey have found their way into the hearts of the whole family. Without realizing it, Maria and Paul have learned something very important: Looking after animals can be a lot of fun, and it has also taught them to be respectful toward other living beings. The two fish feel very content at home with the children who love them very much, and thanks to their care, they will live with them for many years!

Let's go fishing

Material: Bucket, water, wooden or plastic sticks, fishing thread, string, paper clips, corks, templates, hard transparent plastic, washable markers, permanent markers, cleaning rag, scissors, hole puncher.

The fish

1. Draw the outline of the fish with washable markers on the plastic; if you make a mistake, you can wipe it off with a rag.
2. Paint the fish with the permanent markers and cut them out.
3. Make a hole in the top part for catching the fish.
4. Cut the corks into rectangular shapes.
5. Make a deep cut in each cork to insert the fish.

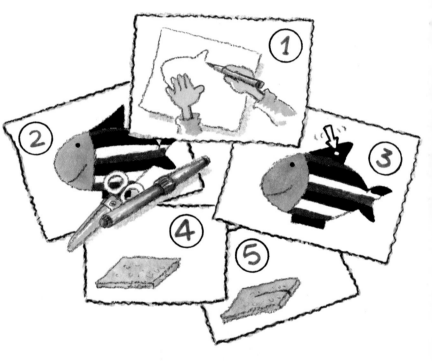

The fishing rods

1. Tie the fishing thread to the end of each stick.
2. Attach an open paper clip to the end of each thread.

Fill the bucket with water. Put your fish in the water, and you are ready to go fishing!

If you write the numbers from 1 to 9 at the bottom of each cork, you can add up the number of the fish you have caught, and the player with the most points will be the winner.

Advice from the vet

THE IDEAL FISH FOR CHILDREN

A wide variety of different fish are available from pet stores for fans of aquariums. The majority require very specific treatment, varying according to the region of the world where each species comes from. Many are very sensitive to temperature, the pH of the water, and the type of food. There are also easier species to care for, suitable for new enthusiasts and also for children. Among these, the goldfish stands out. It is a very hardy fish that can live for many years if it is cared for appropriately.

GUIDELINES FOR CHOOSING A HEALTHY FISH

The goldfish has been bred for centuries, first in China, then in Japan, and finally in Europe, where it was introduced as an ornamental fish. Over time, a great number of varieties have been obtained, with beautiful tails, many different colors, and even strange-shaped heads, fins, and eyes. The most common varieties are the most resilient and they live longer than the more delicate varieties. You should obtain your goldfish from a trusted pet store. The fish you choose should have a healthy appearance and active behavior. You should avoid fish that appear sick and also healthy ones if they share the same aquarium with other sick or dead fish, as they might also be infected.

THE AQUARIUM

Spherical fish tanks should never be used under any circumstances. They get dirty very quickly, and the fish are never comfortable in them. It is very important to obtain an aquarium of the appropriate size, the bigger the better, so that the goldfish will be kept in the best conditions and to prevent stress. The minimum volume of water per fish is 10 gallons (40 L). Also, a strong filter is needed, which while filtering the water, aerates it through a stream of bubbles. The water does not need to be heated, and the ideal temperature is between 64° and 68°F (18° and 20°C). Although fish can tolerate temperatures as low as 39°F (4°C), they don't tolerate the warm water of tropical fish tanks, 75° to 84°F (24° to 29°C), very well. With respect to pH, this should ideally be kept close to neutral (pH 7–7.5). The pH and other water parameters can be monitored by taking a small sample to your local aquarium store.

FEATURES OF THE AQUARIUM

The gravel on the bottom of the tank must be dark and not too coarse. You will need to place a layer at least 2 inches (5 cm) deep, if you wish to have living plants in the aquarium. You can add some stones, but be careful that they don't have any sharp edges on which a fish could hurt itself. You can also add a branch. The aquarium should have a cover and a source of light. It's best to use the dim light of one or two fluorescent bulbs. The light should remain switched on for four to eight hours at the most. This can be automated by means of a simple timer. Goldfish love having an abundance of vegetation in the aquarium. As well as feeding on it, they use the plants to seek shelter when they don't wish to be disturbed. You can ask in a specialized store about the most appropriate plant species, as not all are suitable: Some are delicate and grow slowly, so they could quickly disappear, being devoured by your fish.

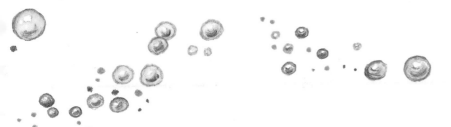

POSITIONING THE AQUARIUM AND CLEANING TASKS

The aquarium should be placed in an area free from air currents, as these can cause sudden temperature changes, to which goldfish are very sensitive. Exposure to direct sunlight should be avoided as too much light bothers the fish. Also, the sun can heat up the water and cause undesirable algae to proliferate and darken the sides of the aquarium. The water should be partially changed often to renew it and prevent the accumulation of toxins. Changing 20 percent of the water once a week is sufficient. It's a good idea to take advantage of these weekly water changes to clean the gravel a bit with the help of a siphon, available from any specialized store. The new water added to the aquarium must be treated with a few drops of water conditioner. This product neutralizes the chlorine and other elements that might be present in the tap water.

FEEDING

Goldfish are omnivorous, that is, their food contains both animal and vegetable matter. There is special food available for goldfish, in the form of flakes, pellets, or powder, which contains all the nutrients the fish need. However, it's a good idea to provide them with vegetable food, in the form of well-washed leaf lettuce, boiled spinach, or special pellets. The goldfish also eat the plants in the aquarium and the algae that grows there. Large goldfish should not be mixed with small goldfish, as the larger ones might bully the smaller ones. It's important not to overfeed the fish. They should be given prepared food (flakes, etc.)

twice a day, and they should finish the portion you give them in about two to three minutes. If there is any food left after this period, you should give them less the next time. It's important to plan the food they will receive when you go on vacation. If you can't find anyone to feed them, there are special foods available for feeding them when you go on vacation.

SIZE AND LIFE EXPECTANCY

By following these simple instructions for taking care of your common goldfish, you can watch it grow up to 6 to 12 inches (15 to 30 cm) in length, and it can live for twenty to twenty-five years or even more. Special varieties of goldfish don't usually exceed 6 inches (15 cm) and don't live as long.

LET'S TAKE CARE OF OUR NEW FISH

English language version published by
Barron's Educational Series, Inc., 2008

Original title of the book in Catalan: *Un pez en casa*
© Copyright GEMSER PUBLICATIONS S.L., 2008
Barcelona, Spain
Author: Alejandro Algarra
Translator: Sally-Ann Hopwood
Illustrator: Rosa Maria Curto

All inquiries should be addressed to:
Barron's Educational Series, Inc.
250 Wireless Boulevard
Hauppauge, New York 11788
www.barronseduc.com

ISBN-13: 978-0-7641-4062-4
ISBN-10: 0-7641-4062-0

Library of Congress Catalog Card. No. 2008926843

Printed in China
9 8 7 6 5 4 3 2 1